There are NO Soulmates!

There are NO Soulmates!

(Give it Up, Get on with Your Life)

M.W.

Ozzbooks

LOS ANGELES

Request for information should be addressed to:
Ozz TV, Inc./Ozz Books
3405 Glendale Blvd., Suite 142
Los Angeles, CA 90039
www.ozztv.net

Ozz Books is an imprint of Ozz TV, Inc.

Layout and Cover Design:
Jen Huppert Design
www.jenhuppert.com

This book is dedicated to my dear friend Lisa
who is a true Soulmate Junkie.
May you find all the love and happiness in the world—
all within *yourself*!

Table of Contents

There are
NO
Soulmates!

Soulmate Junkies

America is a nation of people obsessed with finding their soulmates. Movies are made about them. Books have been written from every angle on the subject, and men and women alike are obsessed with finding their perfect Other, even if it means using online dating services or going on television shows.

We are crazy in love with the idea of finding true love. We have become Soulmate Junkies, hooked on the endless pursuit of finding someone who will complete us.

Are you a Junkie ? Try this simple quiz to see if you too have become obsessed:

Question 1

Do you believe that there's one perfect person for you –your soulmate — someone who'll complete you?

Question 2

Have you put any of your hopes and dreams (your heart's desires) on hold while waiting for your soulmate?

Question 3

Do you believe that your heart's desires will never be realized until you find your soulmate?

Question 4

If you haven't found your soulmate, do you feel like a failure?

Question 5

For those of you who believe you've found your soulmate, do you often find yourself setting unrealistic expectations of your partner/soulmate? Have you ever been disappointed when they don't live up to those expectations?

· ·

If you answered "yes" to any of these questions, you're definitely a Soulmate Junkie! And, if you're a Junkie, you've probably experienced a great deal of frustration, anger, and even disappointment when your efforts to find this person go unrewarded.

Okay, so the word "Junkie" might be a little harsh, but life is too short, and too precious to waste a single moment pursuing an unrealizable goal. Think about how many times you've delayed pursuing any of your heart's desires while you wait for that perfect person to arrive.

Have you delayed traveling abroad until you have Mr. or Mrs. Wonderful to travel with? Are you waiting to buy your dream home until s/he arrives to make the experience "more meaningful?" Have you held onto a bad relationship believing that the person is your soulmate and "they will change" if they truly love you? Have you put any of your dreams—any dream whatsoever—on hold until your soulmate comes?

If you have, then the word "Junkie" is truly accurate in describing your addiction to an illusion.

Why waste all that time and energy?

THERE ARE NO SOULMATES!

So give it up and get on with your life.

The Trap Is Set

The jig is up. There are *no* soulmates. You've been lied to, strung along, and toyed with by those so-called "New Age Gurus." It was all a sham—the big lie.

But, now you know the truth. It's time to move on with the rest of your life and stop waiting for your soulmate—your "twin flame"—to arrive and complete you. Your destiny is now in *your* hands. You are in the driver's seat. Only you have the controls.

There are no soulmates. There's no one else out there waiting to rescue you. There's no one to complete you other than yourself.

What happened to you? Why haven't you achieved your soul's desires—your life's purpose?

Thanks (but no thanks) to this whole soulmate scam, you've been distracted. You've wasted your time. Endless years of waiting for that perfect person to arrive have gone by, and you've only blamed yourself for not finding the perfect other to complete you.

It was all your fault. You were doing something wrong.

Right?

WRONG!

There are no soulmates, so it's time to find and then create the life you've been waiting for...all on your own.

Go ahead. What's stopping you? Oh, I know. You're still clinging to the ideal that soulmates exist, aren't you?

STOP IT, and repeat after me: There are no soulmates. There are NO soulmates! THERE ARE NO SOULMATES!!

This was what I *really* wanted to tell my friend Leeza, a tried and true Soulmate Junkie.

As I sat in an Internet café in Rome reading my emails from America, I read her email. "I'm so glad you're having a good time in Italy," Leeza wrote. "Don't forget to bring my soulmate back to me." I could almost hear her sigh from across the ocean.

I really wanted to tell her the truth. She'd been wasting her time chasing one bad relationship after the next. She really needed to look inside herself to see why she kept making the same mistake over and over. And most of all, she'd never get all those wonderful things she desired—wealth, travel, fine living—unless she achieved them for herself.

But, as usual, I kept quiet and simply replied: "You can cross Italian men right off that list."

I knew firsthand what Italian men were like. No soulmates here, I learned (the hard way). Yes, I had a peek at the truth behind the romantic notions surrounding these Europeans because I had spent several "enlightening" hours with one the day before.

I started the day early—around 7:00 a.m. I was in Rome for seven days, and had a free day and had decided to take a tour to Tivoli to visit the gardens there. The tour was wonderful, but exhausting as hours of hiking and climbing stairs had my otherwise aerobically unfit set of lungs working overtime. It was nearly 3:00 p.m. that afternoon when I finally had a chance to sit down, take a load off my aching feet, and order some food. I hadn't eaten since breakfast and I was starved. Pasta was the perfect prescription.

It was only a minute or two into my late afternoon meal that I realized the waiter was flirting with me.

"You have such beautiful eyes," the tall, red haired Italian man said to me in a sexy Italian accent as he leaned over to serve my pasta (and check out my cleavage).

Okay, so I'm not so sharp. It was an obvious ploy, but at first I thought he was just being friendly to the foreign tourist (that would be me), you know, as part of a foreign diplomacy thing.

The lunch quickly turned into a five o'clock date with the waiter who said he would take me on a walking tour of the city. Normally I'm not one to date waiters in strange countries, but I said to myself, "Foreign country, cute guy, nothing else to do...*when in Rome...*"

Fast-forward to 11:00 p.m. I was desperately trying to shake the young Italian, who, after downing nearly seven beers within our first hour together, had turned into a belligerent asshole (excuse my French). Apparently Italian men like to party hard. They also like to smoke like chimneys, a bad habit that wasn't agreeing with my California health-oriented mentality.

The real fun began earlier that evening (I estimate around 6:00 p.m. or so) when my date began planning our wild weekend of traveling, fun, and lots and lots of sex. It was all harmless fun and flirtation, and besides, I was in the mood for a little Italian romance, so I went along with him and enjoyed the sites of Rome that we were seeing by foot.

Okay, so I admit it. I was quietly wondering, "Is this my soulmate?" It was all very exciting, at least for the first hour.

Back to 8:00 p.m. and the Italian was leaning heavily on my shoulder. He was drunk as a skunk, and I was practically carrying the guy through the back alleys of Rome. As he hung on me, I noticed that he was sweating like a pig, and the sweat combined with his endless smoking was creating a sour smell on what otherwise started out as a fragrant and well-groomed body.

Definitely *not* my soulmate!

"Look, there's a hotel," he slurred for what was now the zillionth time. "Let's see if they have a room. We'll stay there...together."

I stopped dead in my tracks, and gave him the most evil look I could possibly conjure. My diplomatic efforts to explain "American women aren't like that—we don't sleep with people on the first date" (well, in theory anyway) were going nowhere. It was clear he was convinced that through sheer persistence he was going to talk me into having sex with him that night and every night...*for the rest of my long, miserable life!*

"No, no! You no understand. No sex. I just lie there. I won't even touch you," he pleaded over and over again.

Suuuure...

He just wasn't *getting* it, and my arguments were falling on deaf ears. I couldn't shake him. He just kept following me every time I sped up or slowed down. I couldn't yell or scream for help because I was an American woman in the middle of a strange city filled with policemen carrying machine guns. ("We're just used to it," one Italian answered casually when I asked whether Italians were concerned about such displays of force.)

I wasn't about to venture off on my own because by 9:00 p.m. we were in some strange part of Rome. I was lost and starved, so I agreed to have dinner with him even though, at this point, I was ready to strangle the bloke. So we ate our dinner and my dark mood softened somewhat as I watched my date greet the other waiters. He explained that they had been friends for many years, which explained why he had dragged me so far across town: he wanted to show me off to his friends.

It was fascinating to watch these men show such warmth towards one another—a true Italian tradition (or so I've read), and much different from how American men behave.

"It's late. I take you to your hotel. This is a dangerous part of town," he told me after dinner, and I agreed. To be safe, I would let him escort me to my hotel which was situated across from the Vatican, clear on the other side of Rome. We would get there by subway.

"Okay, you can take me, but *you're not staying at my hotel*," I told him, and he was silent. Good! I finally talked some sense into the guy (or so I thought).

Mid-way back to the hotel, he still hadn't said anything. He was thinking...no, *scheming*. I could practically see the gears grinding in his tiny little brain. He wasn't about to give up on his wild-sex weekend. When we got off the train at the Vatican, he put his new plan into action.

"I'm so tired," he moaned like a big baby. "It's late. I have to work at five o'clock tomorrow morning," he said, rubbing his sweaty forehead for emphasis.

Oh no. Here it comes...

"How much is your hotel? Maybe I get a room and sleep there tonight?"

Oh my Gawd! There it was. Brilliant, and oh so bold. My life passed before my eyes. I saw him knocking quietly on my hotel room door around midnight. The quiet taps turned into closed fisted thuds, and then the screaming, and the crying, "Why? Why? Our love was so beautiful!"

I had to get rid of him now, but how? I had tried everything short of screaming rape to shake the guy over the last few hours, but nothing (within reason) had worked. And now we were passing under the tall, stone Vatican walls with a flight of stairs leading down to my hotel approaching just a few yards ahead.

I knew that once we hit those stairs, it was all over. He would see my hotel, and all would be lost. I was on the verge of panic. I had to make my move. It was now or never.

And so I prayed to the Pope for divine intervention, and the answer came in the oddest kind of way.

I stopped abruptly at the head of the stairs and turned to my young Italian friend. "I can't believe you haven't listened to a single thing I've said all night long..."

"No, no! You misunderstand...," he tried, but it was useless. I was a woman on the edge, and now there were no big crowds, no machine-gun-toting polizia there to stop me from fully expressing myself.

"No, no," I said, holding up my hand to stop him. "I can't believe we're standing in front of the F@#&ING VATICAN and you're still trying to get me to have SEX with you," I shouted so loudly that my voice rang off the stone walls above us.

My words stopped him dead in his tracks (apparently the f-word translates quite nicely). He took several steps backwards as if I had landed a right hook square on his jaw. Eyes wide, he put his hand to his mouth in shock, and whispered, "You just used the F-word in front of the *Vatican!*"

Before I could answer, he bolted in the opposite direction and disappeared into the night accompanied by the very last remnant of my belief in soulmates.

I just stood there for a minute, stunned and amazed. Such a simple solution to a potentially complicated situation: blasphemy.

Worked like a charm.

....

The next day, I chatted with my Italian real estate agent on the phone. (I had come to Italy, in part, to check out a few properties.) We had a lot to talk about since she was also an

American and had lived in California before moving to Italy. I now lived in Los Angeles and was contemplating buying a second home overseas. Italy was at the top of my list.

"What in the world made you want to buy a home in Italy?" she asked me.

"Why not?" I said. I had the means and no one in my life to stop me from living out any of my dreams.

We gossiped about the little quirks that make Italy fun and frustrating at the same time—one of them being Italian men—and then I told her about my experience with my Italian waiter the day before.

"That's very typical of Italian men," she explained. "They chase after American women because they think we have a lot of money, and they think they'll have tons of sex whenever they want it. What's worse, they all live with their mothers and expect their wives to be their slaves while they're out partying with their friends and lovers.

"My best friend moved to Venice," she continued, "and hooked up with an Italian man she thought was her soulmate. She hasn't been able to get rid of the guy since. She's trapped. He wants to know where she is at every minute. It's a nightmare for her, but at the same time, she's afraid of being alone in a strange country."

There it was—the soulmate trap, snaring another innocent victim. When will we ever learn? What can we do to stop this madness?

I could understand this woman's friend feeling lonely and a little vulnerable in a strange country, but at the same time, here I was, in Italy alone living out my dream. I wasn't in the least bit timid or afraid. I never once felt threatened or unsafe, even that night I spent being hauled around town by the Italian waiter. As a matter of fact, I was having the time of my life.

I wasn't sure why this woman remained stuck in this awful relationship with her Italian lover, but I was sure of one thing: there was a quick and dirty way out and I had discovered it quite by accident the night before.

"Boy, have I got the perfect solution for your friend," I said cheerily. "It's not going to be pretty, but desperate times call for desperate measures. We'll start with the Vatican..."

A Pretty Decent Proposal

"Will you marry me?"

It was like music to my ears. Not because it was coming from the handsome prince I had imagined since childhood — the one that would get down on his knees and propose in some fantastically romantic location, and then sweep me away to his castle and forever and ever take care of me.

No, this proposal was different. It was coming from the woman who owned the small boutique where I was about to buy at least one new pair of shoes from the batch of open boxes that surrounded me. I needed a good pair of walking shoes for my upcoming trip to Rome and the Italian countryside where I intended to purchase a second vacation home, I told the women in the shop. And I needed a second pair—something strappy and black—for my fortieth birthday dinner with friends that evening.

"Ah, Rome!" said one woman—the shop's owner I later learned. "That sounds so romantic. My husband and I have talked about going there, but..." her voice trailed off wistfully.

"Do you have kids?" I asked the woman, expecting that this was the reason she and her spouse were delaying their dream vacation abroad.

"No," she shook her head. "No children. We're getting older and we're not sure we want to go through the baby phase."

"I know exactly what you mean. That's why I'm adopting an older child...from Russia," I volunteered. "And now, since many countries have opened up their adoption requirements, even single parents like me can adopt."

I went on to explain how I had never been married (no, I'm not *gay*), but decided that I wanted to have my own family instead of waiting for that "perfect guy." I want my own family, under my own terms. I had no desire to give birth to a baby (that feeling had recently passed out of my psyche, once and for all), and I wasn't in a hurry to get married. I was, after all, financially secure and having the time of my life, so why rush out and spoil it?

"Wow! Lucky you!" said the shop's owner. "Will you marry me?"

We all laughed, and then I said, "Sorry. I've already been promised to my friend Roxanne whose husband thinks we make the perfect couple."

In fact, just a month earlier, I had been teaching my friend Roxanne, a self-proclaimed debutante, how to do some simple home repairs — tasks that her writer-husband, Mickey, should have been doing himself, but for some reason had left undone. The chores included simple things like nailing and painting — chores for which Roxanne had assumed she'd be paying a handyman at least two hundred dollars — two hundred dollars she and her sparsely-employed writer-husband simply didn't have.

"No way!" I told her. "You can do it yourself and I'll even show you how. It'll only take fifteen minutes and it'll be *fun*."

Over an hour later, we finally finished our work. I had to stop myself from laughing as I watched Roxanne struggle with the electric drill and paintbrush. It was like watching a chimpanzee apply lipstick and mascara for the very first time. She had no idea what she was doing, but eventually we finished our work and stepped back to admire it, just in time for Mickey to enter the room to lend his expert opinion.

"Looks pretty professional, don't you think?" Roxanne asked her husband.

"Not bad," Mickey grunted, and went back to his writing in the other room.

"Mickey thinks you'd be the perfect husband for me," Roxanne later told me as we spoke on the phone.

"Husband?" I choked.

"Yeah, I think it's because you're more of a man than he is."

So, there it was. I had become the man—no, the *soulmate*—I had foolishly yearned for since childhood up to the age of thirty-nine. But I was forty now, and crossing over to middle age had changed my point of view. At the age of forty, I was completely self-sufficient. I had money to burn, a beautiful home, a luxury car, wonderful friends, and five healthy cats and dogs. I knew how to cook, sew, paint, wield a hammer and electric drill, and I had become a darn good gardener thanks to the beautifully landscaped garden I had inherited from my home's previous owners.

Life was good, but it hadn't always been that way. It was only in the last two years of my life that things had changed for the better, and the changes all began when I began questioning the very existence of a perfect soulmate.

I hadn't given up on love, or the idea of finding a companion who could bring me new life experiences that I had never had before. Instead, I had changed only one thing: I simply ruled out the possibility that my life would be incomplete without someone else to complete me.

This simple shift in my belief system had changed my life for the better. I was free to pursue the things I had only dreamed of doing with my twin flame, my perfect other, my soulmate, and I was taking advantage of that freedom. I was finally going after all my heart's desires with a vengeance, all on my own, and with no hesitation.

In a relatively short period of time I had achieved many of my life's goals that, previously, I had struggled to achieve year after year, but with no success. I soon realized that I had become the man I had always dreamed of marrying. I had become my very own soulmate—my true heart's desire.

God's Plan For You

I consider myself to be a woman ahead of her time. Long before the Atkins Diet was hot, I curbed my intake of carbs. My friends all called me crazy.

I was also into the New Age stuff long before most people I know. I even developed my psychic abilities using dream techniques I developed all on my own. Over the years I've expanded these abilities into waking life. I use all kinds of psychic techniques, from merely closing my eyes and using pictures in my mind to make my predictions, to scanning people's bodies in my mind to detect illness, and even channeling wisdom from the likes of Jesus and Mary. The list of my abilities and the various techniques I use is a long one, and I worked hard to hone my skills.

I regularly publish celebrity, political, and unsolved crime predictions on *The Sixth Search* (www.sixthsearch.com). As far as I know, I'm the only psychic who publishes regular predictions for the general public to read, criticize, and track for accuracy. It takes a lot of confidence in my abilities to do this, and a lot of thick skin when the accuracy of my predictions is called into question.

Yes, ladies and gentlemen, I would consider myself to be a New Age Guru of a sort, and I would certainly consider myself just as qualified as anyone to challenge the concept of soulmate. After all, I've made enough celebrity romance predictions to see just about everything. Even though I've tossed around the word "soulmate" lightly, I've learned there truly is no special spiritual routine going on between these gorgeous couples. They're just regular people dealing with the day-to-day challenges that most couples experience.

I am a very practical, no-nonsense kind of person, and this attitude extends into my spiritual and psychic work. I believe that everyone's psychic, but that we're just so overloaded with the distractions of daily life that we don't pay attention to our abilities. I also believe that there is love everywhere and that we're never alone, thanks to an abundance of entities that watch over us and guide us from several different dimensions.

I know from experience that it's our connection—our partnership with God—that we should keep as our primary focus in life. The closer we are to God, the more harmonious our relationship with God's plan, the more likely we are to feel the love that emanates from all these other sources.

As touchy-feely as all this might sound, I do not, however, buy into the whole soulmate thing, and here's why:

> By assuming that it is our soulmate who completes us, we are further distracted from our direct relationship with God, and from realizing our own creative dreams. And when that connection is disrupted, and when those dreams are diminished, we can become lost.

This is not a book about Christianity, or the Bible for that matter (I don't even own a copy), but I do believe the Bible is the greatest work of literature for a reason; it holds a great deal of wisdom written by a bunch of very smart people. This great book of wisdom was so good that somehow it managed to be handed down from generation to generation for over two thousand years. That says a lot.

It is, however, the interpretation of the Bible by some very nutty people that has screwed things up in this world. It never fails that some crazy, opinionated religious leader manages to convince a bunch of willing followers to surrender their free will to the leader's own idea of how life should be led (all in the name of Jesus or a myriad of other religious martyrs, of course).

My Aunt Carol is a prime example of a follower led astray. Prior to the recent presidential election, she proclaimed that Jesus told her to vote for Bush. Of course, the medium for that message was her church's pastor! There are many more like her who regularly abandon their own beliefs and good judgement because someone of higher authority told them to do it.

When I recently decided to adopt, I decided to use a Christian adoption agency, for the only reason that their website was the most professional and comprehensive. However, I did request packages from one other Christian agency that looked pretty good too. When both packages arrived, I immediately opened them and took a look.

Both organizations appeared to be somewhat similar in terms of the adoption process and procedures, but there was one very subtle difference in the application that helped me choose between them.

"If you are single, please explain why," read one question on the first page of the application that the second agency sent me. So now I needed to produce an excuse, an explanation as to why I never married, why I had never found my soulmate, just as if it were some kind of sin? I immediately pitched the application in the garbage and made my decision to go with the first agency whose application was far more straightforward (name, address...the usual stuff).

When I attended the initial orientation session held by the Christian agency that I chose I had a chance to speak with one of their representatives.

"So, you understand that I would be a *single* parent?" I asked her. "You're sure there'll be no problems?"

"No, no problem whatsoever," she said, and then smiled.

Relieved and assured that I wasn't going to have to deal with some religious bias against single parents, I accepted the orientation package she handed me and took a seat.

A few minutes into the presentation, I realized that the reason I liked them so much was that they apparently stuck to a fairly nonjudgmental translation of the Bible. At the center of the organization's mission to find needy children healthy and happy homes was one simple proverb:

> "For I know the plans I have for you," declares the LORD, "plans to prosper you and not to harm you, plans to give you hope and a future."
> **—Jeremiah 29:11**

"According to God, adopting a child is not Plan B in your life," the speaker explained to the audience. "It is not a second choice, or a life that is God's punishment for not being a perfect person. You *are* living the Plan A life that God gave you. It is God's plan."

I was surprised that this simple proverb struck me as so profound. It forced me to think long and hard about how I really felt about my life. For the first time, I realized that my chosen lifestyle, that of single woman, was not a punishment for not being "good enough" for my soulmate. I was already living the life I was supposed to live. I wasn't in some holding pattern for my real life...a better life. This was it, and I realized, it was *pretty darn good*!

And so, when I returned home, I completed my adoption application and mailed it in. I had added a new element to the plan I had for my life, and I was excited. In a few months, I would be traveling to Russia to visit a potential daughter, somewhere between the ages of three and eight. It would be a new adventure—one of many new and exciting things I was sure to experience now that I was convinced that I held my destiny in my very own hands.

Be Your
Own Soulmate

There is only one soulmate in your life—only one person upon whom you can consistently rely to deliver your dreams and your heart's desires to your doorstep, and that is you. There will never, ever be anyone in your life with more power than you to so completely influence the level of happiness you experience.

What if having another person is your dream? Why can't you have them if it's what you want, what you pray for day and night? If we have free will to manifest our dreams, then why can't we just force the object of our affection—the man or woman we desire—to be completely cooperative with our own romantic visions?

To put it simply: there are three competing forces at work in our plane of existence that we must consider, and they are:

The Will of God
The Will of Others, and
Our Own Will.

Each of the three is just as powerful as the other, and if any one should contradict the other two in any way, there will be conflict. It is this conflict that in turn leads to difficulty and struggles in our own lives.

Rishi's Story

To illustrate: My dear friend Rishi was obsessed with a young woman named Purvi whom he believed was his soulmate—the love of his life. There would never be anyone better, he believed, because they had a "connection"...they were simply meant to be together forever and ever.

From the very beginning I told Rishi the truth about Purvi. "She's using you, and she's dating at least two other men on the side. And you will never, ever end up with this woman."

"No, no! That can't be right. I have a special feeling for her.

I know she is the one," Rishi told me with desperation clearly in his voice. "I will pray every night for her, and I will be patient. It is our destiny to be together. We are soulmates."

And so Rishi prayed and prayed for a life with Purvi for nearly four years, and I watched and listened in frustration as he told me about his struggles with money, with his career, and life in general.

And every time Rishi called me for a psychic reading he asked the same question, "Will Purvi and I finally be together?"

"No, you won't," I told him every time, and I begged him to re-focus his energy on setting and pursuing goals in other areas of his life. "Stop wasting your time. You cannot influence Purvi's will."

"But, why? Why can't I have her? We are soulmates," he begged, hoping that I would give him the answer he desired.

"Because, there are three forces at work in the universe," I explained. "There is God's will. There is your own will. And then there is also Purvi's will. You cannot bend another person's will without hurting them either physically, psychologically, or spiritually or all of the above. So give it up."

Something about what I had just told my friend finally seemed to click.

"Oh, I've never looked at it that way," he admitted.

From that point forward, Rishi made a concerted effort to

change his habits. He didn't call Purvi anymore. He simply forced himself to stop. It took a great deal of effort on his part, but he did it. Purvi didn't bother to call him either. She had never made an effort before, and she wasn't about to change her ways. This only strengthened Rishi's resolve to cut the connection with this woman once and for all.

Over time, he just got used to not thinking about her, and instead, focused his energies on his career, and on making new friends, both male and female.

As a result, his career thrived. Within a period of three years he went from making a salary of $35,000 a year to $100,000 a year plus bonuses. Rishi estimated that if he hit his goals, he could make nearly double his salary that year— up to $200,000—and finally be able to afford the home that he dreamed of. Not bad for a twenty-six-year-old who just two years earlier thought his life would be over if he couldn't have his beloved Purvi.

Rishi realized that he could now fill his life and his home with the woman he always dreamed of—someone who was as lovely as Purvi, but someone who respected him, and loved him unconditionally.

What's more is that I could finally see the image of that person shining through in his life. He was manifesting a very clear vision that he was finally able to see without the distractions of a frustrating romance that was never really a romance at all.

I urged my friend to look back and remember the mistakes that he made in the past. "Don't get stuck like that again, my dear friend," I told him. "There are many, many wonderful people out there, and it's up to you to make the best choice. You deserve it."

The Will of God

"Hope deferred makes the heart sick, but a longing fulfilled is a tree of life."

—Proverbs 13:12, NIV

Deferring our dreams while we wait for our soulmate is simply a ridiculous concept, and I believe that it goes against God's plan for our lives. Period.

I truly believe that God wants us to live the life that we dream of. This life can be anything we want it to be, and it typically is. (So, as the old saying goes, be careful what you wish for.)

Many people are surprised when I discuss God, as if being a psychic goes against the very nature of religion. Yes, I believe in God, but perhaps not in the same way as a Catholic or Buddhist. Instead, I have a rather scientific explanation that comes from my undergraduate years in college where I studied engineering, mathematics, and physics.

No matter what your definition of God (or perhaps you consider this ruling force to be a Goddess, or the Creator of All That Is, etc.), you may have noticed that there are times in your life that have been particularly challenging and difficult. Perhaps you've attributed this to God's will or just plain bad luck. There are other times when things just seem to "click" and life is good.

I've looked back on my life and analyzed what I was doing during the bad times versus the good. One thing I notice is consistently true is that during the so-called bad times I wasn't living the life that I now believe God had planned for me. As a matter of fact, I was working in a career that was contrary to my very nature. As a result, I did nothing but run up against one obstacle after the next. Without trying, I managed to piss off just about everyone I ever worked with.

Fortunately, I plugged away at my life, and was directed by a series of rather painful blows (by a God force, perhaps?) to where I am today. Nothing could be more different from my life today than the life I imagined when I was in my twenties, and I couldn't be happier about how things turned out. I just wish that I had started sooner, and that I hadn't deferred my own dreams while I waited for that mythical soulmate to arrive.

My Story

I wished and wished for my own soulmate for years, even though I wasn't always conscious that I was doing it. As I neared the age of thirty-nine, even though I had been disappointed by one man after the other, I still held out hope for that one perfect person who would come to complete me.

To my relief, just a few months before my thirty-ninth birthday, my friend Linda (a fellow psychic) heralded the news of my soulmate's arrival. "You'll meet him this September," she predicted.

My own psychic readings held the same promise, and I could even see what he'd look like—tall, fair-haired, and pretty darn handsome. I would meet him through an online dating service I predicted.

Sure enough, I met John at one of those dating services that promised, "Yes, you too can connect with your soulmate using our proprietary intelligent matching system."

On our first date, John and I were both impressed with how compatible we were.

"I guess science really does work," John told me over dinner and drinks, and I agreed.

John was very attractive and he was open to all the psychic

stuff I was into (a rare find indeed!). On the first several dates he seemed sensitive and open. We enjoyed each other's company so much that we rented a cabin in the woods together for a few days. We had a great time, and I was especially impressed that John agreed to let me bring my dog Jasper along for the trip.

Things went along smoothly for nearly three months, until I began questioning John's involvement in an organization called Landmark, which, as I later learned, was actually **est**[1] reincarnated. Apparently several of **est's** members did a management buy-out of the company after **est** was sued by the government and subsequently put out of business. They repackaged their cult into what appeared to be a legitimate corporate training program.

As with most cults, **est** (and now Landmark) was excellent at recruiting very normal people, brainwashing them, and then convincing them to carry out the cult's mission of recruiting and training more members who would pay a hefty training fee. Of course, none of the members were ever paid for their work or time, but they were convinced that they were doing something for the "higher good," so that was okay.

I later learned that John was a perfect example of one of these very smart yet insecure people who were easily conned

---

[1] Werner Erhard's **est** [Erhard Seminar Training and Latin for "it is"] was one of the more successful entrants in the human potential movement. **est** is an example of what psychologists call a Large Group Awareness Training program. Others simply labeled it a "cult" because of its cult-like training tactics.

into what I call "group think" all in the name of spiritual enlightenment or "getting it" (whatever "it" was). His membership in Landmark gave John a sense of spiritual superiority. It also gave him a license to lie to me.

"Never lie to a psychic," I had warned him early in our short-term relationship, "because even if I'm not entirely sure of the details (of the lie), I'll definitely know if something's fishy."

Sure enough, John lied to me about his whereabouts on three separate occasions. He later admitted that he was volunteering his time for Landmark, but because his fellow cult members endorsed his activities (and I clearly didn't), he felt that it was okay to lie by omission. As a matter of fact, it was me who was being so unreasonable by daring to question his participation in this supreme organization.

Being the individual free thinker that I am, I ended our relationship quickly, after just three months. Even though I was convinced I had made the right decision in ending things, it was tough to let go. He was my soulmate after all, and I felt as if I had lost my one and only chance at true happiness.

Did I make a mistake? Weren't we meant to be together? Will I ever find that kind of attraction again? Do I need to compromise myself—my beliefs—to be with my soulmate?

After giving it some thought, I realized that I had fallen into the ol' soulmate trap. I simply read too much into our sexual attraction. I also realized that during our relationship, I had compromised my own heart's desires in order to satisfy what I felt my soulmate needed for his own happiness.

For example, prior to meeting John I had come to the conclusion that I simply didn't want to have babies. I was nearing forty and I was busy running my own company and working on lots of fun, creative projects. Sure, I saw myself with one or possibly two children of my own, but the idea of adopting an older child was much more appealing to me than giving birth. John, on the other hand, wasn't open to the idea. He wanted his wife to bear his children, and that was that! So I reconsidered my position on bearing children, even though it went completely against my grain.

Fortunately, I soon realized that I had been sucked into the whole soulmate thing, and that I had been a fool. If I had continued down the path with John as my significant other and the goal of an impossible life of perfection, one of us was sure to compromise—and I suspected that person would be me.

No, I wasn't willing to compromise. I wanted (and deserved) to live the life that would make me supremely happy. Then it dawned on me that perhaps I was already living this life—the life that I was meant to live. This perfect life didn't include John, and that was perfectly okay with me.

The Will of Others

There are certain laws in this country and in other countries around the world that simply must be followed lest we be thrown in jail. There are physical or scientific laws that have been proven to be true, and many more that are still unproven, yet widely accepted to be true. Finally, there are also certain spiritual laws that we must follow as well.

"Do unto others" is a prime example of a spiritual law that has proven to be true throughout the ages. This law implies that if we do good works and work together in cooperation, life will be good and flow smoothly in return. When we work in contradiction with others, or try to bend the will of others, there is conflict and difficulty. It's as simple as that.

In theory, the concept of a soulmate—our other, the one who will complete us—implies that there is one other person out there for us who will work in complete cooperation with us so that we might achieve our goals and realize our heart's desires. In theory it's a great concept, but in reality it hardly ever happens, because every single person on this planet has a will of his or her own.

Roxanne's Story

My friend Roxanne is married and is a stay-at-home mom to her two-year-old child. Her husband, Mickey, is a Hollywood writer, which means his employment status is usually in flux. While he is working steadily, he's typically not making a great deal of money—that is, until he sells his TV pilot. Unfortunately, the odds of selling a pilot are about one in a million.

The couple first met when Mickey rented an apartment from Roxanne who owned several units in a trendy part of Hollywood. They became fast friends and remained that way for several years, until one day Roxanne suddenly became attracted to Mickey, much to his surprise. Roxanne quickly seduced Mickey, and a few weeks later their son, Shaun, was conceived. They married a few weeks later.

To many, Roxanne and Mickey were an accident waiting to

happen. There couldn't have been two people more opposite each other in many respects. One huge difference between the two was their relationship with money. While Mickey enjoyed his Spartan starving-writer's lifestyle, Roxanne was a spender and dreamed of being married to a rich Hollywood husband.

Shaun arrived in the couple's lives at the most inconvenient and challenging time possible (but isn't that the way children always arrive?). Mickey's career was in it's usual "waiting for the big deal to close any day now" mode, and Roxanne was forced to sell her only source of income at the time—her apartment building—so that the couple could live off of the proceeds until Mickey's riches rolled in.

The couple lived like kings on the six-figure-plus profit from the sale of Roxanne's building, and a year and a half went by. Every day, Mickey promised Roxanne that the money was on its way. "We just have to be patient," he told her.

Roxanne waited and waited, but she was getting nervous. Had her handsome prince failed her? No, she wouldn't lose faith. He was the man, and he would surely hit it big any day now...

They continued to live what many would consider to be an extravagant lifestyle complete with a nanny, a housekeeper, two cars, and a rented home that cost nearly $3,000 a month (a lot of money considering Mickey's part-time salary was barely that much). The money went fast, until one day it was *completely* gone. That was when Roxanne came to me for help.

"What can you do to change him?" she asked me, expecting me to wave my magic wand and get Mickey off his butt to find a second job, or a job that paid better than his current part-time position.

"I can't change him, but let's talk about you. Why can't you find a job?" I asked her.

"Well, who will watch Shaun?" she argued.

"What about Mickey? He's only working a few hours a week, you said, so what's the problem?" I replied not wanting to let her get off so easily.

"Mickey says he doesn't want me to work."

"Well, it looks like he has no choice now, doesn't it? You're behind on your credit card payments, you have no money, and now you're borrowing from your parents. You can't keep this up forever, and it's clear that Mickey's not going to change."

It was true. Roxanne had tried and tried to get Mickey to pick up a second part-time job to supplement the family's income, but he simply refused. Roxanne was just as inflexible, and their marriage slowly deteriorated to the point where they were talking what-ifs about divorce.

"Roxanne, you know that you are destined to be the real bread winner in your family," I told her one day, months later.

"You're right, that's what my therapist tells me too," she

finally admitted. "Hollywood did a real number on us with all this handsome prince stuff, didn't they? I guess I'm going to have to face the fact that I'm just stronger than my husband."

Here, here! It was like music to my ears to finally hear Roxanne speak out loud that pure truth: There is no soulmate there to save you. You must save yourself. (It only took over a year and a half of trying to convince her, but better late than never.)

After that I helped Roxanne put together a resume, and she finally sent it in to a company her brother had been begging her to look into for months. I knew that she would get that job, and I knew she would be excellent at it.

"The first few weeks will be tough," I told her, "but you'll do just fine. And just think, by this time next year, you'll have plenty of money to buy a home of your own!"

I was sure that things would work out for Roxanne and Mickey as long as she continued to move her own life forward towards her hopes and dreams instead of relying entirely on her husband to fulfill them for her.

More important, I knew that by going back into the workforce she would set a good example for both her husband and her son. I hoped Mickey would step up to the plate and take on a more active role in providing for his family, but if he didn't, at least Roxanne would have the security she always longed for...all on her own.

Your Own Will

There is nothing as powerful as your own will in shaping the quality of your life here on earth, especially if you are working in partnership with the will of God.

When you are living your soul's purpose—your heart's desires—you are working in partnership with God. And when you are doing this, life suddenly becomes very *interesting*. You'll be challenged to look inside yourself and find strength to pursue your goals, and when you look, you will find an abundant supply.

When you do this, your need to find an external soulmate

to fill your empty spots will disappear. You will become your own soulmate.

What if you don't know what your soul's purpose is? How do you discover your seemingly elusive heart's desires?

Try this simple quiz that I call "The Five Second Life:"

The Five-Second Life

(Note: You can also try a version of this quiz online at http://www.precognito.com).

Life #1

Begin by imagining that you can live an entire lifetime in just five seconds. In that lifetime you can do only one thing—the very thing that makes your heart sing, gives you goose-pimples, and makes you want to laugh out loud.

Close your eyes.

Can you picture it in your mind?

Got it?

Now, write it down here:

_____

_____

_____

_____

_____

(HINT - Don't worry! In this test, you'll live FIVE of these five-second lives, so this first lifetime doesn't have to be perfect.)

$\mathcal{L}$ife #2

Okay, let's do that again.

Clear your mind of Life #1 and let's move on to Life #2. Imagine yourself looking into a big crystal ball. Look inside and see yourself living the life you've only dreamed of in just five seconds.

This lifetime goes fast, so make sure it's a good one. Think of the one career you can do, or just one crowning achievement, or anything you want or deserve.

What does this lifetime look like?

Can you picture just one thing you desire with all your heart?

Got it?

Great! Now, write it down here:

_____

_____

_____

_____

_____

(HINT - Having problems picturing something? Don't worry. It can be anything you desire, and it doesn't have to be in great detail. It could be as simple as "being a famous writer" or "falling in love.")

#3

Okay, now that Life #2 is finished, it's time to move on to the next five-second lifetime. Go ahead. Try a life that's completely different from the first two. You can do anything you want, so look into your crystal ball and get ready...

What do you see?

_____

_____

_____

_____

_____

Life #4

Picture your next life in your head, except in this lifetime you are tasked with learning an entirely new profession as a sorcerer's (magician's) apprentice. This sorcerer will teach you anything you choose.

What will it be?

_____

_____

_____

_____

_____

ℒife #5

Once you're done with lifetimes #1 through #4, take a good hard look at this lifetime. What do you *wish* you could do in this lifetime, but haven't?

Write it down here:

_____

_____

_____

_____

_____

(**HINT** - *If you can't think of anything, that's okay. If you made it through the first three or four lives, you should have enough information to begin piecing together your heart's desires.*)

Your Heart's Desires

Now that you're done with this quiz, take a look at your answers.

These are your heart's desires (or, your soul's purpose) in this lifetime.

Think about each of the things you wrote down. If you can find a way to creatively combine the various attributes of each of your dream lifetimes into one in this lifetime, you'll be well on your way to fulfilling (and living) your soul's purpose. If you listed things like "fall in love" or "spend more time with the kids" or even "be rich" (all very legitimate desires to have), consider what you must do to achieve them, and don't wait. The more you delay pursuing these desires, the more likely you are to become discontent and even desperate for a quick fix (like buying into the whole soulmate thing!).

> Remember: It's important to recognize and acknowledge the talents that you've been given in this lifetime. Think about how you can creatively use these talents when pursuing your heart's desires.

Example

To illustrate how I used The Five Second Life to find my own heart's desires, here are my answers to the quiz questions above:

Life #1:   Be rich.

Life #2:   Be a writer.

Life #3:   Be a private detective.

Life #4:   Be in love.

Life #5:   Have my own family.

When I stepped back to analyze my answers, I realized that I had set aside my own desire to be a writer. I also realized that my psychic ability (a talent I had been given, but never really used before) combined with my interest in unsolved crime was an excellent source of material for a book series.

I had always dreamed of being rich, but when I pursued other types of careers that didn't involve writing and unsolved crime, I seemed to continually hit dead-ends. As soon as I committed myself to being a professional writer, new opportunities arose in my life that began to produce a fantastic income. This new income afforded me the time (and money) to commit to my writing projects.

In the meantime, I began to truly love what I was doing. My work was fulfilling, and my dream to be rich was becoming a reality. I didn't feel the overwhelming need for the love of another person since I truly was happy and felt all the love I'd ever need in this lifetime. As a matter of fact, I had a surplus of love to give to others.

Eventually, I realized that I was in an ideal position to adopt my first child. Even though I would be a single parent, I had a home-based business so there would be plenty of time to commit to my new family. And, since I was making a good living, I had all the money I needed for extra in-home childcare.

Developing A Plan

You may be asking yourself, "Now that I know what my heart's desires are, what do I do with them?"

Good question. The answer is simple:

> Pick a life plan, *any* plan, and lay it out in detail on paper. Then go for it, one baby step at a time until the momentum builds. If it's not the right plan, you'll be directed by God's will in the right direction that is your heart's desire.

For years, I struggled for money and love until, by accident,

I stumbled across the book *Think and Grow Rich* written by Napoleon Hill, which was originally published prior to the turn of the century. Its principles still hold true today, and I encourage everyone to read it. The book's publishers have even developed a workbook that I highly recommend as well.

The key ideas from the book that I applied to my own life are based on the book's "Six Ways to Turn Desires into Gold." I've amended them here into my own six steps for taking your heart's desires and developing them into a workable plan.

Follow these simple steps and you'll be on your way towards realizing the heart's desires you discovered in the previous section's Five Second Life quiz.

Six Steps Towards Realizing Your Heart's Desires:

Step 1

Set a specific goal for yourself, and fix your mind on it. Be sure to be as specific as possible. For example: "I want to have a million dollars in my bank account within the next five years." Don't use generic phrases like "I want the highest and best amount of money." Be specific, including the date or timeframe within which you wish to achieve your goals.

Step 2

Determine exactly what you intend to give in return for the goal you desire. Be prepared to make the necessary steps required to reach your goal. *You must apply effort or you simply won't go anywhere!*

If it is an education you need, then get it. If you need to ask your husband to watch the child while you work a full time job during the day (as in Roxanne's case, for example), then do it. Don't expect money or the things you desire most to simply fall into your lap. You have to apply the brain, talents, and creativity God gave you along with the effort required to reach your goals.

Step 3

Create a definite plan for achieving your desire and then carrying it out. You'll never reach your goal for getting to where you want to be without a plan. Keep in mind you may need to adjust this plan as you go along. (Note: It's important that you develop a fairly detailed plan for achieving your very first big goal. If you need to, pick up a book on writing business plans and use this basic model for your own plan.)

(**HINT** - *Don't have a plan? Make one up!*)

Yes, that's right. If you don't know how to make a specific plan to achieve the various aspects of your heart's desires, then just make one up. Start simple and then expand the plan as your confidence builds.

For example, if you know one of your heart's desires is to be rich, yet you're $30,000 in debt and earning an income of $18,000 per year, perhaps you should focus on developing a plan to pay off your debt first. Maybe this plan entails getting a part-time job, or maybe you'll need to further your education or learn a new trade to earn more money.

No matter what, you can rest assured that your creative choices are never wrong, and they will provide forward momentum towards your true heart's desires.

Step 4

Take action immediately. Put your plan into motion right away whether you think you're ready or not. I'm not saying you should quit your day job. Just devote a few minutes at a time, and then more time as required as you move forward.

Don't worry about making mistakes. There are no mistakes in life. If your plans veer off course, you will be re-directed by your higher self to the path of least resistance, which is usually the direct path towards your heart's desires.

Step 5

Be patient and flexible and most important, keep the *faith*. Realize that "Rome wasn't built in a day," and there are human limitations (and the will of others) that may delay the achievement of your goals. However, it is important to trust that if you pursue your heart's desires, you are in fact living out your soul's purpose. Have faith that God wants you to live a wonderful and prosperous life, and stick to it. You will achieve your goals.

Step 6

Create new goals as you go along. Once you achieve your original goal or heart's desire, add new ones as often as you'd like. This may require that you write another plan for achieving them, or simply develop a plan in your head. It's up to you to determine the best approach.

Example

One of my heart's desires was to be rich. As my business grew (a business, by the way, that I started with only $300 in my bank account), I could certainly see the realization of that goal on the horizon, and I was satisfied. However, since I like to push the envelope, I decided that I would focus on a new goal: I wanted to be *wealthy*.

I developed a picture in my mind of what the word "wealthy" really meant to me. Part of that picture included owning at least one beautiful home in Europe. Subsequently, through a dream, I saw that I would actually own several homes in Europe and perhaps other parts of the world too.

"Where should I start?" I wondered. I picked the most

exciting place that I could think of at the moment: Italy.

After several months of viewing Italian properties on the Internet, I finally found one that I could purchase with the cash that I had saved ahead of time for just this occasion. Sure, the property was a major fixer-upper (I believe the correct word for this type of property is "ruin"), but that was okay with me. It would be fun to renovate an eight-hundred-year-old property.

I contacted the real estate agent and scheduled an appointment to view it on my first trip to Italy.

Cut to the chase: The property was even more gorgeous in person (albeit in worse condition than I had imagined), so I asked the agent to email me an offer agreement. When I returned to Los Angeles I would sign the agreement and make my offer official.

As soon as I returned home, I checked my email for the agreement, but instead, there was a note from the Italian agent's assistant. The property had been sold to someone else. My plan of action had failed. Or, had it?

A few days later, I spoke to a friend who was a financial consultant in the mortgage business. "Forget Italy," he told me. "France has a much more stable economy. That's where I'd buy if I were you."

I began checking out properties in France. There was an abundance of international real estate websites devoted to the country, and the variety of homes, estates and even castles was impressive. Better yet, the prices were competitive, if not better than Italy.

So I adjusted my plan. I'd make a quick trip to France in a few months, but this time I would be able to afford an even bigger property. I began to imagine myself living in the beautiful French countryside in an old castle surrounded by rolling vineyards and horses. I pushed the envelope on what I had previously imagined. Instead of a small, stone, tiered house in a hilltop village like the property I had visited in Italy, I now wanted a big estate complete with all the modern amenities. No ruin for me!

Happy with this new goal, I laid out a plan for getting to France, and put it into action. It would require more work, more money, more time, and a lot of creativity on my part, but I knew I could do it. I was excited and motivated to get there. I realized that had I not chosen to at least give Italy a try and investigate properties there, I might not have been re-directed to France and the world of new ideas and possibilities that began brewing in my brain.

Manifesting Your Plan

Once you've determined your heart's desires, and you've laid out a life plan aimed towards achieving them, it's important that you actually visualize yourself achieving very specific things in your life. I call this manifesting.

I learned this technique from a woman named Viana, but there are lots of different ways to do it. Adapt it to how you feel comfortable.

I use this manifestation technique at least twice a year as I set up new goals for the months ahead. As the year progresses, my plans may shift slightly, but I really stick to the plan that I've laid out for my business and my life.

Manifestations

1. Begin by sitting comfortably in a chair in a quiet place.

2. Close your eyes.

3. Imagine a ball of golden light about the size of your skull, hovering three feet above the top of your head. Imagine that the ball of light is attached to the top of your head with a cord.

4. Now, project yourself up into that ball of light. Imagine a miniature version of your body encapsulated in the ball, staring back down on yourself seated in your chair.

5. Now that you're "up there" in that ball, say the following command:

Father/Mother/God/The Creator of All That Is (or anything you'd like here), I command that

_____

(insert specific manifestation here). Thank you. It is done, it is done, it is done.

6. Once you've commanded your subconscious that your manifestation is, in fact, a reality, look back down on yourself from up there in your little ball, and visualize yourself achieving the goal you desire.

7. When you've visualized the goal you wish to manifest in its entirety, imagine the ball of light you're in is

washed clean with sparkling light. Then pull yourself (and the ball) back down into the top of your head.

8. Open your eyes.

Note

It's possible that you may not be able to manifest your goal(s) within a specific timeframe, but be as specific as possible anyway. Don't worry if you don't hit your mark. The general rule of thumb is that when you put a thought out into the universe it always returns. If you continually expand your thinking, you could receive the fruits of your vision in a much bigger and better form.

Examples

To give you an idea of some of the things you can manifest (the sky's the limit of course), here are a few things I'm working on for 2005:

1. Purchase a castle in France.

2. Publish two books. This is book number one of two.

3. Double the size of my marketing business.

4. Complete the adoption of my first child.

5. Purchase a larger home in California.

When I did my manifestation of the above goals, I followed the steps listed above. For the first item on my list I said, "God, I command that I purchase a beautiful home in

France within the next twelve months. Thank you. It is done, it is done, it is done."

Then I visualized myself purchasing the home (for a really great price, of course), and I even pictured the details of the home (how big it will be, the style, the condition, and other amenities). I felt the excitement in my heart when the deed to the home was handed over to me. All in all, I was as specific as possible.

There will be a great deal of work involved in physically manifesting these goals of mine, and of course, I have a realistic plan to get there. The good news is that I will have little time left to mourn over "where is my soulmate?" I expect that in my travels I will meet lots of interesting people, perhaps one of which will share similar interests and goals, and become a life partner. If not, I won't ever feel incomplete, and I certainly won't delay my dreams.

A Big
Manifestation Don't

As a general rule of thumb, your manifestations will be most effective when you work towards things you control directly and that benefit only you. Examples might include: making a million dollars within five years, buying a new car, etc.

They do not work effectively when you attempt to bend the will of another person. When you try to do this, you run the risk of really pissing the other person off. Witches used to be burned alive at the stake for attempting to manipulate other people, so you should avoid this at all costs.

However, if you do have a life partner or a family unit who

are all in agreement as to a goal to be manifested, it is perfectly all right to manifest a goal for each other. Remember that everyone must be in agreement, but if there is contention, there will be conflict, and ultimately, failure.

The Story of Leeza

My long time friend Leeza is a born-again New Ager. She has also just turned forty, and has been desperately seeking her soulmate since her first exposure to Cinderella and other fairy tales at the age of three. Over the years, Leeza's desperation for finding her soulmate has only increased along with the number of her ex-boyfriends.

Never married, Leeza has committed her life to finding the perfect guy who will bring her the things she's always desired: wealth, travel abroad, attention, the ability to quit her job and work full-time for charity, and a big sailboat.

After a series of major disappointments, Leeza finally snagged a guy named Joe, and they dated seriously for nearly two years. During this time, Leeza began to pursue various business ventures that I was certain would turn into good business for her. One of these ventures was a dinner club for charity that quickly sold out and was a smashing success.

Now Joe wasn't exactly the guy that Leeza envisioned, but Leeza wasn't concerned. She could *change* him. And so began Leeza's quest to bend the will of this poor chap so that he could become her true heart's desire.

Almost out of the blue, Leeza and Joe's relationship began to deteriorate...quickly! It appeared as if Joe had a renewed interest in his ex-wife, and was spending more and more time with her and their young daughter. Leeza was slowly edged out of the picture, but she was determined to wait it out.

"He'll just work it out of his system, and we'll be back to where we were before," she told me. "All I need to do is pray, and I pray every single day that Joe will come back to me. He's my soulmate, so he *has* to!"

Sure enough, Leeza prayed and prayed that Joe would come back. She even joined a New Age church and learned their version for doing manifestations.

"It's what I want, so I know I will get him back," she told me, despite my warnings that it was a very bad idea.

While Leeza was focusing all this energy on getting Joe back, her business ventures disappeared. Despite the success of her charity dinner parties, she dropped the project altogether.

"I just wasn't making any money," she told me when I asked her what had happened to them.

"Why don't you just increase the price, or maybe you should keep more money for yourself instead of giving it all away to charity? That way, you can work full time at it."

"No, no...," was all she said in reply.

A few months later, Joe was gone once and for all. Leeza

had finally given into the fact that he simply wasn't coming back. She was alone, and absolutely miserable. She had been laid off from her full-time job, and since she had abandoned the charity business venture that had gone so well, she was empty-handed and desperately looking for a new job.

Leeza finally grabbed a job as a mortgage broker and was miserable. When I encouraged Leeza to pursue the dreams she had abandoned, she shrugged them off.

"I *will* find my true soulmate!" she told me. "And, when I do, maybe I'll pursue some of those things again."

And so the cycle continues to this day. Leeza is still miserable and clings to the hope of finding a handsome prince who will deliver her dreams on a silver platter.

Cutting The Cord

Many years ago, I developed a really great technique for cutting off relationships that simply aren't serving me any more. This is an excellent technique to use when you're attempting to break off a romantic relationship, but it also comes in handy when you know a job situation isn't working out, yet you're finding difficulty in pursuing new opportunities that could perhaps serve you better.

I call it "cutting the cord," and here's how it works:

Cutting the Cord

1. Sit quietly in your favorite place and close your eyes.

2. Imagine yourself connected at the gut (stomach) to the person or job situation you wish to eliminate from your life. Imagine that there is a cord connecting each of you. Picture it clearly in your mind.

3. Now take a giant axe and cut that cord. (This might actually feel painful, but it's important to cut it clear through.)

4. Once the cord is cut, imagine the person (or entity with which you wish to detach) drifting off into the distance until they disappear. If you need to blow them away with a big breath of air, do it! (This too may feel painful, but it's important to feel the pain and let it pass through you and away into the distance.)

5. Repeat as often as you need to.

When I first began using this technique to break away from bad relationships in my life, it would typically take me one to two weeks before I could easily let go of the other person without feeling emotional pain. Now I'm so good at it that I can easily cut the cord within a day or two and move on with my life without regret or sadness.

Why should you use this technique or other techniques like it? It's important to clear away any emotional baggage so that you have a clear path towards achieving your heart's desires. By doing so, you'll have more energy, and will clear the way for new opportunities and people to enter your life.

Beliefs That Block Us

If you have problems visualizing a goal, it is possible that you may have a belief system that is blocking you.

Unfortunately, many of us believe that life is about sacrifice and punishment, thanks to various misguided teachings of organized religions. "God punishes us for our sins" and "we must make great sacrifices" are common beliefs instilled in us from childhood thanks to Bible-slamming religious leaders, intent on making sure we understand what lowly sinners we are in the eyes of God.

Unfortunately, fairy tale soulmate stories like Cinderella

and Snow White who both suffer on their way to being saved by their handsome prince, and even misinterpretation of Biblical events like the crucifixion of Jesus, have left a very large portion of our population convinced that self-denial is required before being rewarded with happiness and love. Unfortunately there are no guidelines as to when we've suffered or sacrificed enough, so we just keep on doing it.

During all this suffering, many of us simply stop living our lives for ourselves. Instead, we live for the dream of the future...a future that will never come. We begin living for someone else's life, and completely lose sight of our own heart's desires.

When do we stop suffering and start living?

The time is now!

But what about all this suffering? Isn't it required in order to advance our souls? Doesn't God want us to suffer?

Absolutely not!

How do I know? What makes me so sure that this is true? I got the answer straight from " the Man."

The Story of James

My friend James is a television producer for a popular home improvement show on cable. His work requires a lot of long hours and hard work, but James is young, and willing to put in the extra effort required to carve out a lasting career in an otherwise cut-throat industry.

When James came to see me, he was dog-tired. He was losing sleep from all the stress and anxiety in his life. He also felt empty. His dream was to produce documentaries, but he had no spare time with his current workload. And he was lonely. He wasn't really dating anyone special, and wanted to know when his soulmate would arrive, so he came to me for answers.

Rather than perform the typical psychic reading for my friend, James agreed to do a little belief systems work with me to determine whether he was storing any negative beliefs in his body that were producing blocks to achieving his goals.

This belief system work—sometimes referred to as DNA healing—is somewhat complex, so I won't get into detail here as to how it works. Suffice it to say, James and I quickly determined that his belief that he must sacrifice for love/money/etc. was creating a great deal of struggle in his life.

The really great thing about this line of work is that it allows the psychic practitioner (that would be me), to identify and then pull or replace any negative belief with a positive belief. As simple as this sounds (and it is very simple and highly effective in terms of changing unhealthy belief systems without years and years of therapy), I'm always amazed at the resistance people have to making any kind of change in their lives. This was particularly true of James and his belief about sacrifice.

"We must suffer. We must sacrifice. That's what they say in

church. If I don't suffer, I will be going against God. Look at Jesus. He died on the cross, so I need to suffer too. If I don't, my soul won't advance," James argued.

"I don't think that was Jesus' intent when he sacrificed himself on the cross, and I really don't think God wants you to suffer," I tried to argue, but James was sticking to his guns. There was no way he was going to defy what he believed was Jesus' message to him lest he burn in Hell for all of eternity.

"Okay, let's try this," I said after a moment's thought. "Let's go directly to the source. Let's ask Jesus what he thinks about all this?"

"Okay. Why not?" James agreed after a moment's hesitation. What could it hurt?

Now, I had never actually channeled Jesus or any of the Saints or Apostles up to this point but, in theory, they were just as accessible as anyone, so I closed my eyes, went into my psychic mode, and asked the question, "Hey Jesus. What do you have to tell James about his belief that sacrifice is necessary for soul advancement?"

It was a mere fraction of a second before the answer literally popped out of my mouth. I didn't have to think, and I didn't need to ask twice. The answer was clear and simple:

"The people who killed me believed that too."

That was all I had to say.

"Okay, I get it," James said. "I don't need to sacrifice anymore."

....

I am always amazed at how powerful this belief system work is in affecting change in people's lives. Once key beliefs are pulled and replaced with a positive, it's only a matter of days before noticeable changes occur.

This was certainly the case for my friend James. Just two weeks following our session, I met him for coffee, and he looked great. Gone were his blurry eyes and dark circles. He was energetic and optimistic, and had finally started working on his documentary project—just a few minutes a day to start, but it was something.

James also had a new girlfriend. Well, actually, he had known her from work and had contemplated asking her out on a date, but had never followed through. Now that he had more energy (and time too, it seemed), James was dating her, and life was good.

I could see that James would probably not marry this woman, but he was certainly enjoying life. I was thrilled that he was finally pursuing his dream of producing and directing his own documentary. I was certain it would be a success, and life would be good as long as he remained true to his heart's desires and stayed away from this eternal suffering and sacrifice crap.

I also urged him to relax a little on the soulmate thing. "Enjoy dating and focus on creating the life you desire for yourself.

The rest will come naturally," I told him. And so, he did.

Karma

There is one major advantage to being psychic—I always (okay, usually) know the outcome of my own romantic relationships just as they're getting started, although some might consider this to be a negative.

"Why would you want to know the outcome before it even happens? Won't it spoil all the fun?" they ask me. "Doesn't knowing your future create a self-fulfilling prophecy?"

"Yes and no," is what I tell them. "Yes, we have a great deal of control, or free will, over our lives in that we can manifest our heart's desires. However, we cannot control the will of others, let alone the will of God."

Besides, knowing that a relationship is ultimately doomed has always helped me to terminate the relationship at the appropriate time, instead of dragging it on through days, weeks, or months of emotional turmoil. It saves a lot of time, energy, and heartache, I've found.

For example, two years ago I hooked up with a high school friend of mine that I hadn't seen in over twenty years. In high school, Tad was voted class flirt and was widely considered one of cutest guys in school. Twenty years later, my high school chum was still cute as could be, although a bit weather worn from countless hours spent on the golf course during his days as a golf pro in Florida. And, he was still a flirt—big time!

For our one-on-one reunion, Tad and I met for Sunday brunch, which quickly turned into a walk on the beach, cocktails, and then dinner. We talked for hours about high school, and entertained the thought of dating again after all those years. Tad had been divorced twice, and I was never married, so why not? There was nothing to stop us. After wrapping up our dinner, we made plans to get together the following weekend. We kissed good night and drove off to our respective homes.

Once home, I raced inside to give my prospective romance a little psychic spot check (I am, after all, very psychic and use this talent in all aspects of my life from predicting romantic encounters to picking the best mutual funds). I pulled out my handy tarot cards and threw ten of them out onto the carpet. I studied the cards to get an idea as to how long this relationship was destined to last.

Was Tad my *soulmate*, I wondered.

"Damn! Two weeks!" No, Tad was clearly not my soulmate, and if the cards were right, a mere fortnight was all we had, but why?

As I studied the cards, I could see the complications in Tad's life. There were his ex-wives (both of whom apparently still had designs on their former husband). Clearly, Tad wasn't over them either. And there was more. There was yet another woman...a younger woman that Tad would eventually marry. Wife number *three*!

Not one for wasting even two weeks, I made the best of the time Tad and I had together. We had dinner, went to a Jimmy Buffet concert, and had sex (a welcome relief from a dry spell in my life that had lasted nearly a year). It was fun, but when Tad's calls stopped coming, I knew why, and that was okay. I didn't waste time blaming myself (What's wrong with me? Boo-hoo!) and I didn't try to call Tad for closure. It was over, and I moved on. Still, I had to wonder why there was so much passion there during our first meeting and the two or three dates we had afterwards.

Simple: It was the strong memories of our past life together—our junior high and high school past life, that is.

Tad and I had grown up together, and we still remembered the best parts of those days gone by. It was the familiarity and nostalgia associated with time gone by that fueled our brief romance, but fun as it was, it wasn't enough to last. Tad and I were simply much different people now—far too different to be life partners at this stage in the game.

I'm a firm believer in past lives that extend beyond this lifetime. I believe that we often meet people (both men and women) in this lifetime that we've known in a previous life. And, as was the case with my friend Tad, there's usually a great deal of excitement and déjà vu associated with these meetings. The mistake we make is assuming that this rush of emotions and anticipation is the universe's way of saying "Guess who's coming to dinner? It's your *soulmate*, here to help you fulfill your karmic destiny."

I blame Hollywood for putting us, especially us women, into this frame of mind. They tell us, "Your handsome prince(ss) is coming to save you. Now, s/he may not be perfect, but it's important that you work out these karmic obligations that you have with one another. *It's the only way your soul will advance.*"

"But how will I know him/her?" you might ask.

"You'll just *know*," the New Agers say.

"So, what can I expect when s/he gets here?"

"Oh, it'll be great. Your soulmate will teach you an important lesson or maybe even a bunch of lessons. We're not sure exactly what they are, but rest assured, you'll learn something. Or, maybe they'll complete you—you know, fill in those empty spots that you feel all over. Or, they could be your twin—you know, your other half. They will be the One. Oh, and if you're lucky, you might even be in love and have great sex."

"But, why can't I just learn those lessons on my own?"

"We're not sure..."

"And, where in the Bible does it say that I have to have a relationship with a soulmate for my soul to progress? I thought it was all about knowing God, not some other poor human soul like me."

"We're not sure the Bible says anything about soulmates..."

"And, what if I don't feel empty? Then what?"

"Oh, you feel empty. *Everyone* feels empty...and incomplete."

"Okay...if you say so..."

"Thank goodness you've got a soulmate out there waiting to help you. You clearly don't know what you're talking about!"

Right.

• •

There's karma, and then there's *karma*. Some know karma as the "do unto others" principle. In other words, what goes around comes around. If you act like a jerk, you'll be punished somewhere along the line. It's simple physics.

Some New Agers extend the definition of karma to include relationships from past lives brought forward to the current lifetime to be resolved. These, often painful, karmic relationships (according to the New Agers) usually include relationships with one's soulmate. I disagree that soulmates are (by someone's definition anyway) karmic relationships that we must work out while on this earth.

The best definition of karma that I've ever heard came from a famous healer and channeler named Viana. During one of our training sessions, I asked her about her own definition of karma, and this is what she told me: "Karma is merely the memory of other people that we've met in our past lives. There's no contract that has to be fulfilled, no pain or suffering with this person required in this lifetime. It is merely a memory, nothing more, and nothing less."

"But, what about all this pain and suffering and relational experiences the New Agers say is required for our soul advancement? Don't we need that? Isn't that what karma is all about?" I asked Viana.

Viana merely laughed and said, "It's all hogwash."

I tend to agree. Don't scientists say that it's always the simplest explanation that holds the truth? Hasn't all this karma stuff made making life decisions, especially romantic decisions, needlessly complicated? And do we really need karmic relationships for our soul to advance? Monks have been practicing in a vacuum for centuries and haven't their souls advanced?

I've been single all my life and I would consider myself to be a pretty great person. I'm very enlightened and closely connected to God. I regularly manifest great things in my life, and I'm surrounded by a great deal of love and beauty. There are no karmic lessons that have a stranglehold on my life. I admit that I am constantly learning lessons through circumstances and the challenges that I choose to take on in my life, but they're not unduly difficult or frustrating. Instead, they pass into and out of my life with ease.

What Viana had to say completely made sense. This complicated karma stuff just seems so *ridiculous*!

Nonetheless, Viana did qualify her statement: "The general karmic principles of doing unto others in this lifetime still apply, so don't forget it."

A Quick Note About Sex

There are a number of other beliefs that are emblazoned into our psyche that I feel provide barriers to pursuing and achieving our heart's desires. One of these ridiculous beliefs is that sex is love.

It's very easy for us to misinterpret sexual attraction and compatibility for love. But, sex is *not* love, although it is an *expression* of love. Don't confuse the two, and be conscious of this rule when evaluating a potential partner.

If you find yourself attached to someone that you truly should get rid of but are finding it difficult "because the sex was so great," be sure to use the cutting the cord technique as often as you need to. If you remain attached to someone with whom you have an intense sexual obsession, you run the risk of draining energy from pursuing your heart's desires. It's a classic trap; so remember, sex is NOT love.

Soul Groups

I recently attended a party with a friend of mine. I didn't know anyone there, but I made my best effort to mingle. The first couple that I spoke with was a brother and sister. She introduced herself as an architect and he was a doctor from Florida.

"What do *you* do?" she asked me.

"Well, amongst other things, I'm a writer. I'm currently writing a book titled *There Are No Soulmates*."

The couple was stunned. I would best describe the young man's facial expression as one of a person who had just watched me kick a cute puppy to death. To put it simply: they were horrified.

"How exactly do you define the word soulmate?" the man asked me with an accusatory tone in his voice.

"I think there are a number of different definitions of soulmates out there, but I'm addressing the concept of 'the one perfect person who will complete me.' I simply think it's unrealistic and even irrational," I responded to this man of so-called modern science.

"But what about love? Are you saying that it doesn't exist?"

"No, not at all. I'm just saying that we shouldn't heap so much importance on finding a perfect being to complete us. *We* should complete ourselves," I tried to explain, but from the expression on his face, I could tell that he had already tuned me out.

We chitchatted uncomfortably for a few seconds more, then with the "I need a refill" excuse, we all moved to completely opposite sides of the party.

After a quick visit to the cocktail bar, I spotted my friend who was standing with a couple who appeared to be husband and wife. I quickly made my way over to them, hoping to be rescued with a round of lively conversation. I was soon engaged in a conversation about Italy with the woman, whose name was Diana.

"I'm trying to convince Tim to move to Italy," she told me.

"Oh? What region?" I asked.

"Sorento...But Tim's not convinced. He's a homebody and loves it here in Los Angeles. So we've decided that I will spend four months there putting together a plan for both of us. If he doesn't agree to the plan, we don't go, although I can't fathom the idea of not living there. If he does, well, I'll be thrilled. I just love Italy and I'm ready for a change. I've been working as an editor for the museum's publications for years, and now I'm ready to do my own writing. I'm ready to live the dream. But...I'm afraid Tim won't go for it, and I'll have to give it all up."

"I'm positive you'll come up with a creative solution that will be work for the two of you. After all, you're both in the art industry, and Italy is a hotbed of culture and fine art. There are an infinite number of creative possibilities for both of you in your lives, and if you seek it, you'll find it," I told her, and her face literally glowed with excitement.

"Oh, I'm so excited to meet you," she replied. "I was so concerned that I'd come to this party and meet a bunch of the same old people, but you're a true soulmate!"

I had to laugh to myself at Diana's casual use of the term soulmate, but also wondered whether I had been some sort of messenger sent to encourage her to pursue her heart's desire. Perhaps the word soulmate should have a broader definition than the definition that true aficionados of the more romantic "one and only" version hold close to their hearts.

Do we just need a little encouragement along the way to realizing our heart's desires? Are there others who will help us to reach them?

Death & Life

I first encountered the concept of soul groups in my dreams. Much of my unsolved-crime psychic work is done in my dreams using a technique I developed, quite by accident, many years ago. I also use my dreams to predict my own future, including how and when I will die. During this particular dream vision, I experienced my death and what lies beyond it.

I regularly use my dream work to help others, but I also use it to help myself by sometimes looking backwards in my life to childhood and sometimes forward into my future. My predictive dreams have never been wrong and it's exciting to watch them unfold in real life. Dreams of my childhood have also been amazing in terms of helping me to understand why things are the way they are in my life now.

One night in my dreams, just for the heck of it, I decided to look forward to my death. "How will I die?" I wondered, along with "When will it happen?"

In my dream, I could see that I would die of pneumonia around the age of eighty. I estimated my age based on the age of my son who was in his thirties in my dream. (During the time of this dream, I had no children whatsoever, so it was interesting to see that there would be at least one child in my life, and in this case, a boy. I now predict that this child will join my life somewhere around the year 2009 or 2010.)

As I crossed over from life to death, I could see myself attached to my body with some kind of cord. I tried to hold onto the cord and my life on earth, not because I was afraid of dying, but because my son was having difficulty with his marriage at the time and I felt I needed to stay here on earth to help him.

I held on as hard as I could until I heard a voice telling me, "It's okay. He'll work it out all on his own. He doesn't need you anymore."

And then this person or entity showed me my son's future, and a great sense of relief washed over me. I let go of the cord that held me in this plane of existence and dove deep into what appeared to be an ocean. When I came out on the other side of this deep ocean, there was a group of people waiting there for me.

I was so excited to see these people—these very old friends of mine—and I experienced a sensation of complete and utter love for them that I've never felt here on earth. We talked with one another about our experiences, and we even joked about how silly we'd been during different phases in our lives.

"See what you did there?" one friend asked, pointing to a section of my life that we were watching through our minds' eyes. "You were such an *idiot*," she said, and we laughed wholeheartedly at my foolishness.

It was great fun, and I was completely ready for my next experience. I had no lingering longing for life on earth, and I knew that I would see my son again somewhere down the road. Maybe we'd meet again in the next life, maybe not, but since time didn't exist, I knew it would be a mere moment. No matter what, I felt that it had been a great honor to have him as a child in my cherished lifetime back on earth.

When I woke from my dream I realized that I had encountered my own soul group. I was very excited that I had a group of spiritual friends who were always with me, always rooting for me during difficult experiences that would help me learn valuable soul lessons.

"Have I ever met these people here on earth?" I wondered. Sure it was possible, I thought. I certainly believed that my son will, at some point, chose me as his mother (and I him), but I wasn't convinced that consistent soul group experiences were a hard and fast rule for learning lessons and advancing our souls while here on earth.

Considering the rather small size of my soul group versus the sheer population of humans here on earth, I suspected that the odds of meeting all or even one of them here on earth were pretty slim. Besides, wouldn't my seemingly supportive soul group want me to mingle and make new friends during this incredible experience on this unique plane of existence, especially considering that they're always "there" anyway?

Yes, I think they would, and so would I.

Soul Playmates

My neighbors—Richard and Suzanne—are a lovely, creative couple living a life that truly reflects their hearts' desires. She's a costume designer for famous rock stars and for movies and television. He's a Shakespearean actor who spends his summers in Oregon performing in the theater. In the off-season he heads back down to Los Angeles to pick up work in commercials and television. They have been together as a committed couple for nearly three years, and they were recently married. Neither Suzanne nor Richard believes in soulmates.

out of my system during my last
was a complete disaster," Richard told
of a soul playmate much better."

Richard went on to explain that he believed that life is like a giant sandbox. "As we play, we meet other people who are willing to play along with us. When the play stops being mutually beneficial to both parties, we can choose another playmate, or play along by ourselves."

I like Richard's idea of a soul playmate. It implies a certain level of cooperation for the play to continue without confrontation. As with children, when one party stops working and playing well with others, the problems start and the opposite party has a decision: stay and be miserable, or leave to play alone or find a better playmate. The latter requires a leap of faith that there is a better life out there, somewhere.

And then there are those lost or misguided children who don't know what in the world they want to do while hanging out in the sandbox. Should they play with the ball, build a sandcastle, or is there something better to do on the other side of the sandbox? While this type of child sits there deciding, another child comes in and snatches the ball. Another takes away the shovel and bucket to build his sandcastle. Yet another child pairs off with a fourth child, and they decide to play patty-cake.

All the while, the lonely, uncertain child sits all alone and

wonders: "Where is my playmate who wil
me happy? I'm *bored*."

Life doesn't have to be boring. Our part...
be dull (as we might want to label them). It's up to us to live
life according to our heart's desires so that we can create
situations that attract our perfect playmates if that is what
we desire. If our playmate chooses to play with someone else,
that is okay. There's an entire sandbox filled with other
playmates willing to play along with us. When we prefer to
play alone, we play alone, but we will never actually feel alone
as long as we are occupied with the play that we love. It's as
simple as that.

What's Next?

When I recently emailed my friend Joanne to tell her that I was writing a book titled *There Are No Soulmates* she wrote, "Too funny. It is so true and makes me feel better about being alone for sure."

It broke my heart to read her note. I knew that Joanne had been struggling since childhood with autoimmune disease and a number of allergies, so a great deal of her energy was dedicated to maintaining her own fragile health. However, she had managed a number of long-term relationships that simply didn't work, mostly because they required more energy than Joanne could spare.

To think that Joanne blamed herself or felt that ᵤₕₑ was a second-class citizen because she didn't have a soulmate made me wonder how many people in the world believed the same thing. As far as I was concerned, no one—not one single person in this world—should ever feel less of a person for not being part of this fictional soul pair.

Despite the fact that I'm clearly shooting down a hallowed romantic concept here, my hope is that readers of this book will walk away with a more optimistic view of life.

> You can get what you desire in life all on your own because you are already the complete person God intended you to be. You have absolute freedom to realize your dreams—you don't have to put them on hold while you wait for someone who doesn't even really exist.

When I recently traveled to Italy, the beauty of the sprawling gardens, the sculpture, art, and architecture astounded me. It gave me pause to think about the centuries of amazing men and women who pursued their dreams of beauty and luxury long before the concept of soulmate became as popular as it is today. They survived quite well without the ideal of a soulmate to live for. Why can't we?

Fast-forward to 2005. American life is filled with electronic gadgets, gas-guzzling cars, and prefab homes completely devoid of any art or architecture. The ideal life for many of us consists of a husband and wife (soulmates of course), one or two children, and a laundry list of silly things that add nothing more than convenience and noise to our busy lives.

Yet, we're still so unhappy with ourselves. We wallow in the big-screen visions of soulmate perfection, and remain dissatisfied with our everyday lives, spouses, boyfriends or girlfriends.

Has the concept of soulmate really served us that well? Are we better off waiting endlessly for that perfect person to bring joy, beauty, and happiness into our lives instead of creating that life on our own? Considering the modern cookie-cutter American way of life, I'd have to say "no."

I am my own soulmate. I have my own dreams for myself and for my adopted children when they arrive in my life. I plan to teach them that they are perfect and complete in themselves. I will make sure they know what their true hearts' desires are and that they follow their plan to achieve them. I will also teach them that there is love everywhere, and that they deserve to have it all. They will also know that if they want a soul partner, it is up to them to become the person they wish to attract.

I hope that you will try the different techniques I outlined in this book to find your heart's desires. I hope that you will pursue them, master them, and change your life for the better. It's time to stop torturing yourself with silly dreams that pale in comparison to the life you can create for yourself.

May you realize that you already have all the love that you will ever need in this life and the next. May you have a lovely life.

I did it all myself. You can too.

What the heck—you deserve it!

About The Author

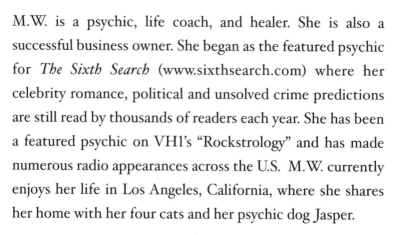

M.W. is a psychic, life coach, and healer. She is also a successful business owner. She began as the featured psychic for *The Sixth Search* (www.sixthsearch.com) where her celebrity romance, political and unsolved crime predictions are still read by thousands of readers each year. She has been a featured psychic on VH1's "Rockstrology" and has made numerous radio appearances across the U.S. M.W. currently enjoys her life in Los Angeles, California, where she shares her home with her four cats and her psychic dog Jasper.

Coming Soon...

Women are Whores/ Men are Idiots
Healing the Spiritual Rift between the Sexes
M.W.

Self-Help

Have you ever wondered why men and women are so different? After thousands (if not millions) of years on this planet, we've evolved into spiritually enlightened individuals. Nonetheless, we still don't completely understand one another. Men and women are simply different creatures by nature. Or, are we?

M.W. is back with a new take on the battle between the sexes. This time, M.W. channels messages from Jesus and Mary, God, and various Spiritual Guides in an attempt to discover the true spiritual role of the sexual divide. In *Women are Whores/Men are Idiots* M.W. will explain why this spiritual gap is no longer useful, and what you can do to mend your soul and your relationships with members of the opposite sex.

Coming Soon...

The Touch of Love
M.W.

True Crime

M.W. puts her psychic crime-solving skills to the test in this real-life story of how she discovered the hidden truth behind one of the biggest serial crime sprees in U.S. history. If you are a true crime enthusiast, *The Touch of Love* will challenge your belief in the accuracy of current police and FBI methodology. This book also provides a unique insight into the psyche of serial killers and how their parents and society create them. It also takes a unique look at the souls of these career criminals.

OZZbooks

Make A Better Future For Yourself. GET A DEGREE!

Did you know that Bachelor's degree holders earn 64% more than those with only a high school diploma? (U.S. Dept. of Commerce) Master's degree holders earn even more.

Search for convenient career college programs in your area at College911.com (http://www.college911.com). Request your FREE INFORMATION today.